FAVOURITE

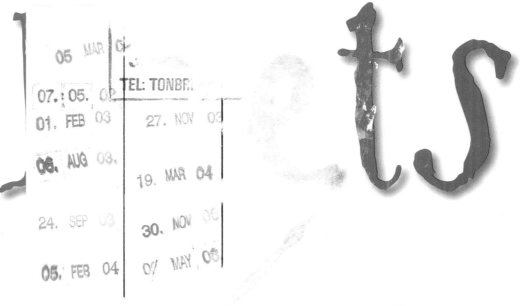

ts

by Brian Moses

Titles in this series:

favourite Poets
favourite Writers

Text © Brian Moses 2000

Editor: Sarah Doughty
Designer: Tessa Barwick

This edition published in 2000 by
Hodder Wayland, an imprint of
Hodder Children's Books

Cover permissions: (top left to bottom right): *Fruits* by Valerie Bloom, artwork by David Axtell,
reproduced by permission of Macmillan Children's Books, London; photo supplied by Valerie
Bloom; *Smile, Please!* by Tony Bradman, artwork by Jean Baylis; reproduced by permission of
Puffin, imprint of Penguin Children's Books; photo of Tony Bradman supplied by Egmont
Children's Books; artwork by Claire Mackie, from *Michael Rosen's Book of Nonsense* published
by Hodder Wayland; main photo supplied by Roger McGough, *Bad Bad Cats* by Roger
McGough reproduced by permission of Puffin; photo supplied by Judith Nicholls; *Someone I
Like* by Judith Nicholls, artwork by Giovanni Manna, reproduced by permission of Barefoot
Books; *Talking Turkeys* by Benjamin Zephaniah, artwork by Janet Woolley, reproduced by
permission of Puffin.

A Cataloguing record for this book is available
from the British Library

ISBN 0 7502 2791 5

Printed in Hong Kong by Wing King Tong

Hodder Children's Books
A division of Hodder Headline Ltd
338 Euston Road, London NW1 3BH

Contents

Valerie Bloom

Valerie Bloom was born in Clarendon, Jamaica, in a small village called Orange Hill. With eight brothers and sisters she never had any trouble finding someone to play with, and the family house would often fill up with various cousins who came to stay. Rhymes from the skipping games that she played sometimes appear in the poems that she writes today.

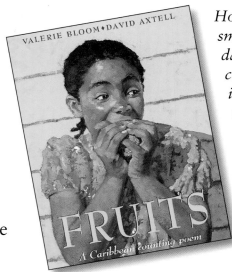

How much fruit can one small girl eat in one day? This Caribbean counting poem introduces the reader to counting numbers and the names of Caribbean fruits.

Autumn Gilt

The late September sunshine
Lime green on the Linden Leaves,
Burns bronze on the slated rooftops,
Yellow on the farmer's last sheaves.

It flares flame-like on the fire hydrant,
Is ebony on the blackbird's wing,
Blue beryl on the face of the ocean,
Glints gold on the bride's wedding ring.

A sparkling rainbow on the stained-glass
*   window,*
It's a silver sheen on the kitchen sink,
The late September sunshine
Is a chameleon, I think.

From: *Let Me Touch the Sky*
(Macmillan, 2000)

Valerie started writing stories as soon as she could write but only started composing poetry when she was in her late teens. Her first poem was published when she was 19. The music and the rhythm in poetry always fascinated her, "Once I found I could reproduce the rhythms and feelings I was hooked." She came to England in 1979 and a collection of poems for children, *Duppy Jamboree*, was published in 1992.

SELECTED BIBLIOGRAPHY
Duppy Jamboree (CUP); Fruits; New Baby; Selected Poems (Macmillan).

Your Questions . . .

Why do you write poetry?

Because I have to. The feeling of exhilaration I get when I've finished a poem is quite addictive. I get into a very bad mood when I'm unable to write.

Where do your ideas come from?

Everywhere and anywhere. Ideas come when you look, listen, taste, smell, feel and touch and they are all around. I read as much as I can, speak with and listen to people – especially other writers, and try to be acutely aware of everything around me.

Where do you write your poems?

On trains, in hotel rooms, in libraries, in the garden, in bed, in the kitchen, in the bath, in my study, at parties, weddings, funerals . . .

How do you write your poems?

I use a pen and paper for the drafts, before putting the final version on computer. I write down all my ideas very quickly and then start to shape the poem. Occasionally I start writing what will be the finished poem without sorting ideas because that's the way the poem comes to me – occasionally.

What is your favourite book?

Mine – *Fruits*. Someone else's book: *The Top 500 Poems* (ed. William Harmon).

What is your favourite poem?

It changes. 'Fruits' was my favourite for a long time. At the moment it is 'Sandwich'. Who knows what it will be next year? There are so many poems that are favourites. Among them are 'The Listeners' (Walter de la Mare), 'The Road Not Taken' (Robert Frost) and 'Rough Riding Tram' (Louise Bennett).

Tony Bradman

Tony Bradman lives in Beckenham with his wife, three children and a tired word processor. "My home is in south London and isn't that far from where I was born in 1954." Tony read a huge amount when he was a child, and spent a lot of time playing games that involved a lot of fantasy and imagination. He also liked to talk and enjoyed playing with words and listening to songs (particularly the Beatles) so it was a natural progression for him to start writing. He was in his mid-20s when his first poem was published in a magazine.

Grandad

My Grandad's tall,
And very thin,
And everyone says
I look like him.
But I haven't got a wart
On my chin. . .
My Grandad drives his car very fast. . .
ZOOOOOOMMMMMMMMMM. . .
Toot! Toot!
Squeeeeeeal. . . Zoom, Zoom
ZOOOOOOMMMMMMMMMM. . .
That's him, going past.

Extract from: *Smile, Please!* (Puffin)

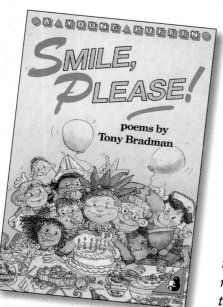

Full of poems about the ups and downs of home and school life, this book is ideal for those beginning to read poetry for themselves.

Tony's first children's book was published in 1984 and he has now written or edited well over a hundred books of both poetry and stories, making him one of the top 20 children's authors.

SELECTED BIBLIOGRAPHY

Smile, Please! (Puffin).

Anthologies: Off to School; The Hairy Hamster Hunt and Other Pet Poems; Here Come the Heebie Jeebies (Hodder Wayland).

Your Questions . . .

Why do you write poetry?

There are some things you can only say in a poem; images, ideas, thoughts that have to be expressed in the form of a poem and cannot be brought to life in any other way. Also, there is real pleasure simply in playing with words and rhythms.

Where do your ideas come from?

Everywhere. From memories, things I see, or hear, or experience, or read about, people I meet, places I go. The poem 'Grandad' was inspired by my grandfather-in-law, who also drives very fast!

Where do you write your poems?

I do most of it in my study at home. But sometimes I write in the kitchen, which is a big sunny room, and sometimes I sit outside in the garden with a notebook. I've written some of my favourite things out there.

How do you write your poems?

The same way I write everything. A flash of inspiration, an idea, a vision of the whole poem's overall shape and structure followed by lots of hard slog as I try to realize that vision in the specific words of the poem (or story). Lots of thought, lots of re-writing and revision, lots of struggling until it feels as if I shouldn't do any more.

What is your favourite book?

Smile, Please! (Puffin) because so many of the poems in it were inspired by my own children. Another favourite is *Please Mrs. Butler* by Alan Ahlberg, although I'm a big fan of Kit Wright, Grace Nichols and Jackie Kay.

What is your favourite poem?

'Grandad'. I always read it on my school visits and get everyone to join in the chorus (Zoooooommmmm!). My favourite poem from another writer is probably 'Who?' by Charles Causley.

Charles Causley

Charles Causley has lived all his life in the town of Launceston in Cornwall where he was born in 1917. He attended the village school and then returned there to teach after six years in the Navy during the Second World War. The War was perhaps why he started writing poetry. "You can't write novels and plays on the lower-deck of a destroyer, but you can write poems in your head."

Charles Causley's collection of magical verse. As well as wizards, ghosts and mermaids he says he has "included poems of mystery and magic many people see in day-to-day events, too."

All Day Saturday

Let it sleet on Sunday,
Monday let it snow,
Let the mist on Tuesday,
From the salt-sea flow.
Let it hail on Wednesday,
Thursday let it rain,
Let the wind on Friday
Blow a hurricane,
But Saturday, Saturday
Break fair and fine
And all day Saturday
Let the sun shine.

From: *All Day Saturday and Other Poems* (Macmillan, 1994)

"All poetry is magic," Charles Causley writes in the introduction to his anthology of magic verse, and the folklore and legend of Cornwall is present in many of his poems along with his great love of the sea. His first book for children was *Figgie Hobbin*. This included many poems that were inspired by his mother's childhood memories. Charles Causley was appointed a CBE for his services to poetry in 1986.

SELECTED BIBLIOGRAPHY

Figgie Hobbin; Jack the Treacle Eater; The Young Man of Cury; All Day Saturday and Collected Poems for Children (Macmillan); Going to the Fair – Selected Poems (Viking); Early in the Morning (Puffin).

Anthologies: The Puffin Book of Magic Verse; The Puffin Book of Salt-Sea Verse; The Sun, Dancing (Puffin).

Your Questions . . .

What made you start to write?

I was always an avid reader and thought that if I could write a book myself, I'd die happy.

Why do you write poetry?

If I didn't, I think I'd explode.

Where do you write your poems?

I go nowhere without a notebook and pencil. Rupert Brooke, the First World War poet, called his notebook 'a repository of ideas that didn't get away'.

How do you write your poems?

Very slowly. I once asked the South African poet, Roy Campbell, how he managed to write such marvellously effective poems. He said, 'With an ordinary lead pencil.'

What is your favourite book?

I have no favourites among my own books but one by another writer would be *A Cornish Childhood* by the historian and poet A.L. Rowse.

What is your favourite poem?

I haven't a favourite in my own work, but I wish I'd written 'Ozymandias' by John Keats.

What do others say about Charles Causley?

"Among the English poetry of the last half century, Charles Causley's could turn out to be the best loved and most needed." Ted Hughes.

John Foster

Size-Wise

Our teacher Mr Little's really tall.
He's twice the size of our helper Mrs. Small.
"Were you big when you were little?"
Sandra asked him.
"I was Little when I was little,
but I've always been big!"
he said with a grin.
"Have you always been small?"
Sandra asked Mrs Small.
"No," said Mrs Small.
"I was Short before I got married,
then I became Small.
But," she added, "I've always been little."
"That's the long and the short of it,"
said Mr. Little.
"I've always been big and Little,
but she used to be little and Short,
and now she's little and Small."

From: *Climb Aboard the Poetry Plane* (OUP, 2000)

A collection of poems about getting out of school at the end of the week – about parents, teachers, holidays and much more.

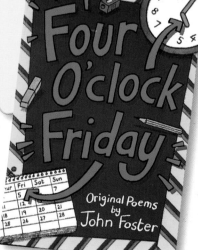

John Foster believes that words should be stretched and twisted till they say whatever he wants them to say. He began by making up rhymes and stories to entertain his two sons on long car journeys. As a teacher, he also started writing poems to use with the children he taught.

John was born in Carlisle in 1941 but he now lives near Witney in Oxfordshire with his wife, Chris. Today he visits schools, and the poems he writes are to entertain schoolchildren. But he also writes serious poems about issues such as bullying and the environment; the kind of poems that will make children think.

John is also a highly regarded compiler of poetry anthologies and many of today's newer names in children's poetry, such as David Harmer, Tony Mitton and Brian Moses, were first published in his books.

Your Questions . . .

Where do your ideas come from?

They come from experience, observation or imagination – sometimes it's a combination of all three.

How do you write your poems?

Once I've got an idea for a poem, I'll start to write the first draft. I'll usually work on the poem for up to an hour. Then I'll stop and leave it till later to do a second draft. I often do the two drafts on the same piece of paper, so it looks very messy with lots of crossings out! Once I've redrafted the poem, I type it up. After that, I'll often make one or two final alterations.

What is your favourite book?

My favourite book is *Four O'Clock Friday* (OUP) which was the first book of all my own poems. My favourite book of someone else's poems is Lindsay MacRae's *You Canny Shove Yer Granny Off a Bus* because it's got lots of poems in it that make me laugh and also some very serious ones.

What is your favourite poem?

My favourite poem that I've written is 'Ten Dancing Dinosaurs'. My all-time favourite poem is the classic poem 'Kubla Khan' by Samuel Taylor Coleridge.

SELECTED BIBLIOGRAPHY

Four O'Clock Friday; Standing on the Sidelines; You Little Monkey!; Making Waves; Bouncing Ben; Doctor Proctor; Bare Bear; My Magic Anorak (OUP).

Anthologies: Dinosaur Poems; Monster Poems; Magic Poems; Crack Another Yolk; All in the Family; School's Out; Excuses, Excuses (OUP).

Ted Hughes

Ted Hughes was born in 1930 in Mytholmroyd, a village in the Yorkshire Pennines. His family moved to South Yorkshire where he attended Mexborough Grammar School and was encouraged to write by his English teacher. His first book *The Hawk in the Rain* was published in 1957.

From 1984 until his death in 1998, Ted Hughes was Poet Laureate, responsible for writing poems to mark important Royal occasions. He was also a farmer and many of his poems were realistic descriptions of the natural world which often gave us insights into ways that human beings behave.

Woodpecker

Woodpecker is rubber-necked
  But has a nose of steel.
He bangs his head against the wall
  And cannot even feel.

When woodpecker's jack-hammer head
  Starts up its dreadful din
Knocking the dead bough double dead
  How do his eyes stay in?

Pity the poor dead oak that cries
  In terrors and in pains.
But pity more the woodpecker's eyes
  And bouncing rubber brains.

From *Under the North Star*
(Faber, 1981)

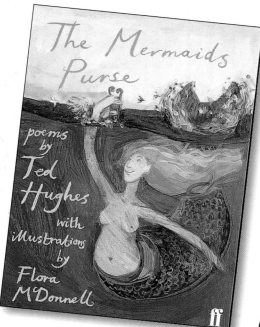

Ted Hughes married the American poet Sylvia Plath, who died in 1963. His second wife, Carole, helped him in the early days of the Arvon Foundation, where courses were held for would-be writers including children at a house in Yorkshire and in Devon.

These poems take you on a journey – from the dark ocean bed, to the beach, and up to the skies. In each location, you find out what it's like to be a sea creature that lives there.

The Poet's Words . . .

"The first verse I ever wrote at school was not for class-work but to amuse some of my class-mates. In my children's books, I simply took up where I had left off at school – as if writing for that same audience, amusing them and myself. When my own children came along, that slightly changed my writing for young people.

My audience was now first and foremost my own children . . . I've written about things that I'm most fond of – birds, beasts, fish and the rest . . . I wanted to hand over a strong, imaginative feeling about their real lives, but also affection.

More generally . . . I've always tried to write, in a way that would excite my young readers and yet at the same time encourage them to say: 'I can do something like this, I have thoughts like this' – as I can remember saying myself. To achieve that effect, while writing as well as you can . . . that's my ideal."

SELECTED BIBLIOGRAPHY

Meet My Folks!; Season Songs; Moon-Whales; A Farmyard Fable for the Young; Nessie the Mannerless Monster; The Iron Wolf: Collected Animal Poems Volume 1; The Mermaid's Purse (Faber & Faber).

Anthologies: The Rattle Bag; The School Bag (both with Seamus Heaney, Faber & Faber).

Roger McGough

Roger McGough was born in Liverpool in 1937. He was about 18 years old when he first started writing poetry. "I remember one night when I just started writing . . . right through till dawn and into the following day. It was a great outpouring to do with discovering myself – not very good, but passionate." This writing began when Roger was a student at Hull University and after he left he worked as a teacher, eventually returning to Liverpool.

Liverpool in the early sixties was being put firmly on the map by rock groups such as the Beatles. Roger formed a group called the Scaffold who performed a mixture of comic sketches and quirky songs such as 'Lily the Pink'. He was still working on his poetry and his first book appeared in 1967.

This was followed by *The Mersey Sound* with fellow Liverpool poets Adrian Henri and Brian Patten. Roger was awarded the OBE for his services to poetry in 1997.

The Missing Sock

I found my sock
beneath the bed.
'Where have you been
all week?' I said.

'Hiding away,'
the sock replied.
'Another day on your foot
and I would have died!'

From: *Pillow Talk*
(Viking, 1990)

The Leader

I wanna be the leader
I wanna be the leader
Can I be the leader
Can I? Please?
Promise? Promise?
Yippee, I'm the leader
I'm the leader

OK what shall we do?

From: *Sky in the Pie*
(Kestrel Books, 1983)

A collection of poems about the exploits of some gangster cats; the verse is based on the music called the 'Carnival of the Animals' by composer Camille Saint Saëns.

Your Questions . . .

Why do you write poetry?

It seems more secretive. A coded message. I enjoy condensing thought and making word patterns.

When did you start writing for children?

. . . I'm not sure I ever did start – at any rate consciously. It's just that all my poetry is intended for the widest possible audience and some of it seems to be OK for kids.

Where do your ideas come from?

From other poems, from my own poems. From mis-overheard conversations . . . association of ideas and words.

How do you write your poems?

I begin them anywhere, but I usually finish them off in my study. (I haven't always had a study – but somewhere quiet.)

How do you write your poems?

In notebooks. I rewrite a lot and put the various drafts into different hardback notebooks.

SELECTED BIBLIOGRAPHY

Sky in the Pie; You Tell Me (with Michael Rosen); Pillow Talk; Nailing the Shadow; Lucky; An Imaginary Menagerie; Bad Bad Cats (Puffin).

Anthologies: Strictly Private (Puffin); The Kingfisher Book of Poems About Love.

What is your favourite book? What is your favourite poem?

These are two questions I always regret answering, because I change my mind from week to week. So let me just say that I have many, many favourites of each.

Wes Magee

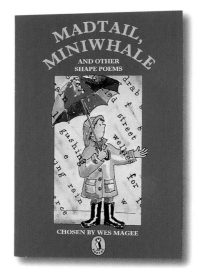

Wes Magee lives in a small village on the North Yorkshire Moors with his wife, Janet, a collie dog, three cats and a very old tortoise. He writes his poems in an old caravan at the bottom of his large garden.

Wes began writing poems in 1969. He was working as a teacher and a boy in his class at school couldn't find any poems about dinosaurs, so he sat down and wrote a set of seven dinosaur poems to fill that gap.

Wes went on to become a headteacher and then in 1989, he became a full-time writer. Since then he has started writing each day at 4 am and believes that the hardest thing about being a writer and working alone is keeping a story or poem going once you've started it.

Above: Poems become pictures in this book of shape poems.

Right: Meet a whole host of spooky characters in this book of raps, rhymes and riddles.

Rhamphorhynchus
(the fish-eating, flying reptile)

Look,
as he swoops from the cliff's rugged face
His squadrons of teeth instant death
To careless fish basking in shallow seas
And lizards short of breath.

His tough skin is cracked and worn as old boots;
His cries blood-curdle the night.
A Dracula beast with claws on his wings
He glides . . . the world's first kite.

From: *Morning Break and Other Poems*
(CUP, 1989)

SELECTED BIBLIOGRAPHY

Morning Break and Other Poems; The Witch's Brew and Other Poems (CUP); Lost Property Box (Macmillan); The Phantom's Fangtastic Show! (OUP); The Boneyard Rap and Other Poems (Hodder Wayland).

Anthologies: The Puffin Book of Christmas Poems; Madtail, Miniwhale and Other Shape Poems (Puffin).

Like many writers, Wes believes that the most exciting part of being a poet is seeing a new book in print.

Your Questions . . .

Where and when were you born?

In Greenock, Scotland in 1939 but I grew up in Yorkshire and Ilford.

Why do you write poetry?

Because I enjoy expressing myself; also I like to organize the world of words on paper; and I do it to earn a living.

Where do your ideas come from?

Everywhere. . . and anywhere . . . and at any time of the night or day. I never get stuck for ideas. They are endless in their variety. A ride on a fairground gave me the idea for a new set of poems. What's it called? *Ghost Train!*

What is your favourite book?

My favourite book from the ones that I've written is *Morning Break and Other Poems*. My favourite book by a

children's writer is *The Castle of Adventure* by Enid Blyton. As a child I found it a gripping, well-described and humorous adventure story.

What is your favourite poem?

'The House on the Hill' (a horror poem) is a favourite out of my poems. My choice of another writer's work would be 'Stopping by Woods on a Snowy Evening' by Robert Frost.

Adrian Mitchell

Adrian Mitchell was born near Hampstead Heath in 1932. Today he lives on the other side of the heath quite near to his birthplace. Each day he walks there with Daisy, his golden retriever.

When he was 14 he began to write something every day, but before that he had been writing funny poems, stories and his first play. He worked as a journalist writing about music, books and television and spent his 21 months of National Service in the Royal Air Force. This must have been difficult for Adrian because he opposes war, but fortunately, at the end of his time he was able to leave having 'killed nobody'.

SELECTED BIBLIOGRAPHY

Balloon Lagoon and Other Magic Islands of Poetry (Orchard).

Anthologies: Strawberry Drums; The Thirteen Secrets of Poetry (Hodder Wayland); The Orchard Book of Poems; Dancing in the Street (Orchard).

Beattie is Three

At the top of the stairs
I ask for her hand. O.K.
She gives it to me.
How her fist fits my palm,
A bunch of consolation.
We take our time
Down the steep carpetway
As I wish silently
That the stairs were endless.

Published as 'Beatrix is Three' from *The Apeman Cometh* (Jonathan Cape, 1975)

Adrian's poems have often concerned themselves with political issues – war and peace, racism, the nuclear debate, but he has also written many poems about his family, his friends and his animals.

An anthology of poems from around the world; chosen because they are sweet – like strawberries, and like drums because all of them have a beat.

Your Questions . . .

What made you start to write?

Because I fell in love for the first time and wrote poems about love every night – and also because I became very puzzled by the way in which terrible wars kept taking place.

Why do you write poetry?

For the love of words, the love of the world, the love of people and animals. It's also my way of talking to people because in real life I'm very shy.

Where do your ideas come from?

My garden, the street, TV, dreams, the papers, my family, conversations overheard on buses and trains, my dog, Daisy. Too many ideas – not enough time to write.

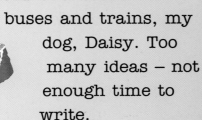

Where do you write your poems?

Wherever I am when the lightning strikes. I rewrite them in a small study.

How do you write your poems?

The first stage is a scribble at speed to get the pictures down on the page. The second stage is a cool stage of rewriting and thinking.

What is your favourite book?

My favourite book of my own is *Balloon Lagoon*. My favourite books by other people are *Songs of Innocence and Experience* by William Blake, *Treasure Island* by R. L. Stevenson and *Huckleberry Finn* by Mark Twain.

What is your favourite poem?

The best poem I ever wrote is 'Beattie is Three' about my daughter. My favourite poem is 'The Tyger' by William Blake.

Brian Moses

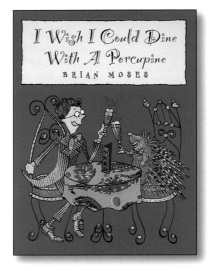

Brian Moses started writing as a teenager. He was heavily influenced by the music of the 1960s and he tried to play guitar and write songs. When he realized that he wasn't going to become a rock star he put the guitar away and the songs turned into poems. Brian became a teacher but he was always being told off by his headteacher because his children spent too much time on poetry and not enough time doing maths!

A collection of humorous and imaginative poetry.

Days

Days fly by on holidays,
they escape like birds
released from cages.
What a shame you can't buy
tokens of time, save them up
and lengthen the good days,
or maybe you could tear out time
from days that drag, then pay it back
on holidays, wild days,
days you wish would last forever.
You could wear these days with pride,
fasten them like poppies to your coat,
or keep them in a tin, like sweets,
a confection of days
to be held on the tongue
and tasted, now and then.

From: *Barking Back at Dogs*
(Macmillan, 2000)

Brian was born in Ramsgate in 1950 but now lives on the Sussex coast with his wife, Anne, and their two daughters. Since quitting teaching in 1988, Brian has read his poetry in well over a thousand schools and libraries from as far north as Scotland to the Channel Islands, and Cyprus.

SELECTED BIBLIOGRAPHY

I Wish I Could Dine With a Porcupine (Hodder Wayland); Don't Look at Me in That Tone of Voice; An Odd Kettle of Fish (with Pie Corbett and John Rice) (Macmillan).

Anthologies: The Secret Lives of Teachers; Aliens Stole My Underpants; I'm Telling on You – Poems about Brothers and Sisters; A Sea Creature Ate My Teacher (Macmillan); The Worst Class in School; Poems About *series*; Poems About Me; Poems About You and Me (Hodder Wayland).

Your Questions . . .

Why do you write poetry?

I love words and the way that poetry allows you to string words together in a variety of ways. I love the rhythms of poetry, and the way that a poem is a snapshot giving you a brief glimpse that is often so powerful that it can stay with you forever.

Where do your ideas come from?

An idea is like a knock on the door. I grab it quickly before it can escape. Many ideas come from listening in to other people's conversations. I once overheard six teachers all telling each other what they wore in bed at night. I made two pages of notes while I was sitting there. This sparked off my anthology *The Secret Lives of Teachers*.

Where do you write your poems?

Initially anywhere – trains, planes, hotel rooms, on the beach. I finish them off in my study which is a room that I had built in my back garden. It is bright with sunlight and looks out over lots of trees.

What is your favourite book?

Often it's the last book of my poetry that has been published. Robert Westall's books rate highly with me but my all-time favourite children's book is *The Brothers Lionheart* by Astrid Lindgren.

What is your favourite poem?

At the moment, my favourite of my poems is 'The Lost Angels' about turtles in a French aquarium. Two of my favourite poems by other poets are 'When you are old' by W. B. Yeats and 'The Horses' by Ted Hughes.

Judith Nicholls

Judith Nicholls feels that her love of words began in early childhood. In the small Lincolnshire village where she spent the first four years of her life she would listen to the frail and ancient Miss 'amby reciting 'Twinkle Twinkle Little Star' or singing 'Now the Day is Over' in a shaky and hesitant voice. In other houses nearby there were nursery rhymes to be shared along with tea and gossip at Aunt Nellie's. The earliest poem that she remembers writing herself was 'Eeyore's Birthday' when she was seven.

Circus Elephant

Today, I dance,
I tiptoe, sway,
with sawdust at my knees;
yesterday, lifetimes away,
I lumbered through the trees.

From: *Storm's Eye* (OUP, 1994)

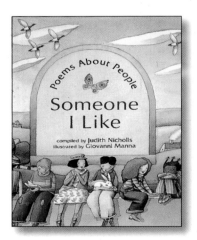

Over the years Judith has worked for a national women's magazine and taught in both primary and comprehensive schools. She didn't begin writing seriously until many years later when she was married and her three children were teenagers. Her first book, *Magic Mirror*, was published in 1985. How did she feel when it was accepted for publication?

"YABBADABBADOOOO!"

Above: A compilation of poems about our friends and family by poets from many different cultures.

Right: Following on from Magic Mirror *and* Midnight Forest, *a book of poems that includes some strange creatures – beginning with the birth of the first dragon.*

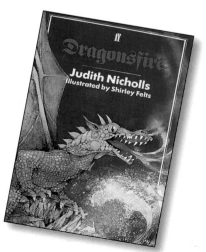

SELECT BIBLIOGRAPHY

Magic Mirror; Midnight Forest; Dragonsfire (Faber); Wish You Were Here; Storm's Eye (OUP).

Compilations: Earthways, Earthwise; Otherworlds; What on Earth …? (Faber). A Trunkful of Elephants (Methuen and Mammoth); Someone I Like (Barefoot).

Your Questions . . .

What made you start to write?

It's hard to say, but when I was young, I was very shy and preferred writing to talking. I also think that everyone in the world likes to make something: a painting, a model, a cake, a table, a dress, a garden . . . I like to take a pile of words and make something from them!

Why do you write poetry and not prose?

I like to spend a long time drafting a poem – trying out many alternative words/punctuation/word order/ways of saying things, throwing out words, bringing them back . . . luckily a poem is much shorter than a novel!

Where do your ideas come from?

Unfortunately, often they don't 'just come' – I have to chase them! However I do try to keep my eyes and ears (and all senses) open for ideas.

Where do you write your poems?

In my study, which used to be the bedroom of one of my children. It's very jolly, with books, paper, pencils and various little treasures everywhere and pictures all over the walls.

How do you write your poems?

Painstakingly!! Force myself to scribble down any ideas that might be faintly useful . . . eventually I set down a very rough 'poem'. I always start with a pencil and paper before moving on to the computer.

What is your favourite book?

I've written about 40 books (if you count all the twiddly little ones too!) but I guess my favourites are probably my own collections.

John Rice

John Rice was born in Glasgow in 1948. His love of words began when he started making up lyrics to instrumental records by The Shadows in the early 1960s. His fascination with space travel and astronomy began about that time and many of his poems reflect this interest.

John is married to Clare and for the past thirty years they have lived in Kent. His first book for children, *Zoomballoomballistic*, was published in 1982 and for many years John has visited schools where he reads his poetry and performs his show 'Eye of Silver, Eye of Gold' – a mix of comic poems, stories and juggling. Many of his favourite stories come from the Western Isles of Scotland. A recent book, *The Dream of Night Fishers* is made up entirely of poems that John has written about these Isles.

SELECTED BIBLIOGRAPHY

Bears Don't Like Bananas (Hodder Wayland); Dreaming of Dinosaurs; An Odd Kettle of Fish, with Pie Corbett and Brian Moses (both Macmillan); The Dream of Night Fishers (Scottish Cultural Press).

Rhyme-osaur

Out of a deep, dark mine-osaur
at roughly half past nine-osaur,
there came a sleepy stegosaur
into the warm sunshine-osaur.
He warmed his chilly spine-osaur
which made him feel divine-osaur.

He nibbled on a pine-osaur
and drank a glass of wine-osaur.
But then he saw a sign-osaur
which made him yelp and whine-osaur.
It forecast his decline-osaur –
his time had come to die-nosaur!

From: *Dreaming of Dinosaurs*
(Macmillan, 1992)

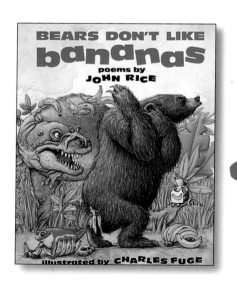

A collection of humorous and zany poems about animals and nature.

Your Questions . . .

What made you start to write?

I enjoyed writing essays and 'compositions' at school and always loved words. We never had books in our house and I had to borrow books from a man called Mr. McGhie – and all he had was a dictionary! An English teacher who like me, had an edible surname (Mr. Melon) once told me, "You're a born writer," and I suppose I started from that point.

Where do your ideas come from?

Mainly from words having accidents. Sometimes you see words bumping into themselves or falling over one another. For example, the other day and I saw an advert for 'photographer' then I saw 'mahogany' outside a timber merchants. Put them together and you get 'mahogany photographer'. . . I like the idea of a wooden person taking photos because you're supposed to stand still anyway!

Where do you write your poems?

I used to write in the living room at 4 or 5 o'clock in the morning when no one was around. I'd sit at the dinner table and write with my favourite pen in a notebook. But nowadays I use the computer. I still sometimes get up at 4 am and start typing up daft poems and laughing at my own jokes!

But the place I love best for writing poems is the Island of Barra in Scotland. It's quiet and peaceful and the scenery is beautiful. The weather's not so good there because sometimes you can have ten days of storms followed by a period of even worse weather!

What is your favourite book?

My favourite book as a child was an astronomy book – *1001 Questions Answered About Astronomy* by J.S. Pickering.

Michael Rosen

Michael Rosen is a real inspiration. He started writing as a teenager and soon discovered, 'the voice of the child he once was'. His first book for children, *Mind Your Own Business* was published in 1974 and his poetry has been a huge success with both teachers and children.

Michael was born in 1946 and grew up in Harrow, Middlesex. Of his work today, Michael comments, "Sometimes I go into schools, sometimes I'm on the radio, sometimes I write, sometimes I lie in bed thinking of all the things I would write if I got out of bed." Some people worry about whether his 'free verse' is really poetry – "If they are worried, let them call it something else, e.g. 'stuff'."

SELECTED BIBLIOGRAPHY

Lunch Boxes Don't Fly; Quick, Let's Get Out of Here; You Wait Till I'm Older Than You!; You Tell Me (Michael Rosen and Roger McGough); Wouldn't you Like to Know?; You Can't Catch Me (Puffin).

Anthologies: Michael Rosen's Book of Very Silly Poems; Mini Beasties (Puffin); Michael Rosen's Book of Nonsense; Michael Rosen's ABC (Hodder Wayland).

Rodge said,

*'Teachers – they want it all ways –
You're jumping up and down on a chair or something
and they grab hold of you and say,
"Would you do that sort of thing in
your own home?"*

*'So you say, "No."
And they say,
"Well don't do it here then."*

*'But if you say, "Yes, I do it at home."
they say,
"Well, we don't want that sort of thing going on here
thank you very much."*

*'Teachers – they get you all ways,'
Rodge said.*

From: *You Tell Me* by Michael Rosen and Roger McGough (Penguin, 1979)

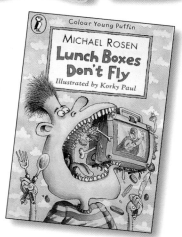

If you love food, then this is a book that you would enjoy; a mixture of old favourites and new poems.

Your Questions . . .

Where do your ideas come from?

Language fascinates me; it is an experience, a place in itself. People always think about what it means, but it's not just meaning, it's sound and grammar. I'm fascinated by how the English language works and 'hangs together'. Really, we all are. That's why we like puns, like 'What's the strongest shellfish? . . . Muscles!' That's language working.

The sound of a word or a phrase intrigues me. I like the word 'video'. It sounds like the rhythm of an Irish jig, so I wrote a jig about a video. Sometimes poems start with a memory . . . for instance, I saw a typewriter recently and it made me realize that you no longer hear them. This started me writing 'The Old Jazz of a Typewriter'. It's a jazz poem about the noise typewriters make.

I often jot down a word or phrase to remind myself to write about an incident that's happened to me. When there is an 'I' in my poems it means that the poem is true. Sometimes it will have happened to me, sometimes to others.

Which three words would you use to describe you and your poetry?

'Spoken' and 'bitter-sweet' – and I can't get the third into one word. It's this way of looking at things from the 'inside out', to get something from a different point of view. To get 'inside' what seems ordinary and making it quite different from what it seemed from the outside.

What is your favourite poem and who is your favourite poet?

The favourite poem is called 'The People, Yes!' and it was written by my favourite poet, Carl Sandburg [a famous US poet 1878-1967].

Benjamin Zephaniah

All You Sea

Three billion gallons
Of sewage
Floating in de sea.
Whales an dolphins
Don't like it,
Seaweed an fish
Don't like it,
De dead at sea
Don't like it,
Zephaniah
Don't like it.

Three billion gallons
Of sewage
Floating in de sea.
There's a time bomb
In our water,
De boats are
Dirty too,
Three billion gallons
Of sewage,
All for you.

From: *Funky Chickens*
(Puffin, 1997)

A thought-provoking collection of poems from the rap poet – incorporating issues such as politics, racism and the environment in its own unique style.

Benjamin Zephaniah lives in East Ham, in East London, next door to the West Ham football ground. He grew up in Birmingham and developed his talent for rap and rhyme at the Deykin Avenue School. Competitions would be held to discover the best rhymer – "Someone would pick a word at random and I would improvize a poem around that word. I usually won."

SELECT BIBLIOGRAPHY

Talking Turkeys; Funky Chickens (Puffin); School's Out (AK Press).

Benjamin started to create poetry a long time before he started to write it down. He admits that he only learnt to read and write properly when he was 21. He loves having fun with words but he also uses his poetry to express his views and concerns. He confesses that he wants to change the world by talking about peace and love. He says "I hate war, I hate armies and I hate guns."

Your Questions . . .

Why do you write poetry?

I feel that it is one of the most direct art forms there is; all you need is a pen and paper; even if you can't write all you need is a couple of ideas. Although I have published a novel, I still love poetry. I hope that people are able to relate to different aspects of my poetry according to their needs. They can get into the rhythm, the anger, the fun or when I perform they can simply try to understand me through my body language and facial expressions.

Where do your ideas come from?

Everyday people inspire me. I am always taking in information from newspapers, TV; from animals and from nature at work. But it's people that are the best. I love travelling and talking to people in various parts of the world; when I listen to their joys and fears I get most inspired.

Where do you write your poems?

I have specially converted my attic to a library-type study where I do most of my writing.

How do you write your poems?

I like to use different techniques when writing – mainly with performance in mind. I work with rhythm and I hear the poem in my head before I write it down or write to a musical beat. Sometimes I write in silence starting with a blank piece of paper. Sometimes I work with rhyme and at other times I like to write free verse. I hate sticking to one style; I love breaking rules!

What is your favourite book?

Hidden Words by Spike Milligan, *Talking Turkeys* by me.

What is your favourite poem?

'The Mask of Anarchy' by Percy Bysshe Shelley is one of them.

Other favourite Poets

Clare Bevan

Clare Bevan was a teacher for years, but now she writes stories and poems for children. She lives in Crowthorne with her husband Martin and her son Benedict. Her best friends are two bad cats called Mycroft and Moriarty and a handsome stick insect called Tutankhamen. She likes to write her stories in a large comfy armchair, with her two cats on her lap but poems can happen anywhere, anytime – in a supermarket queue, on a sandy beach, stirring coffee in a café, or quarrelling with a computer. Her first published story, *Mightier Than The Sword* won the Kathleen Fidler Prize in 1989 and her latest book of poetry is called *Everyone I See is Luckier than Me* (Hodder Wayland).

Paul Cookson

Paul Cookson grew up wanting to play football for Everton and guitar for Slade. He was born in Lancashire in 1961. He started writing songs but then switched to writing poetry. He worked as a teacher at first but now spends his time performing his poetry. Like many writers, Paul is often asked to write poems on different subjects and coming up with something for a deadline – "It's like doing your poetry homework!" Paul's books include *Sing That Joke – Selected Poems for Children* (Solway Books), *Elephant Dreams* (With Ian McMillan and David Harmer, Macmillan), and the anthologies *Unzip Your Lips, Unzip Your Lips Again* and *We Are Not Alone* (Macmillan).

Pie Corbett

If you meet Pie Corbett and notice that there are words written on the backs of his hands, they are there to remind him of poems that he wants to write – and are worked on later in the special room at the end of his house where he sits and writes in hardback notebooks. He writes for children because when children hear poetry they respond well, "Most children know how to listen and to engage with what you are doing, they are able to absorb themselves into the moment far more easily than adults can." Pie's poems are featured in *An Odd Kettle of Fish* (Macmillan) and his anthologies *Custard Pie* (Macmillan) and *It's Raining Cats and Dogs* (Puffin).

John Cunliffe

John Cunliffe once worked as a regional children's schools librarian in Buckinghamshire. During this time he started reading children's books and then trying to write them himself – ". . . an itch to set words on paper, that goes back to my schooldays, when the one thing I had good marks for was for my essays and stories." John, of course, is the writer of the highly successful *Postman Pat* books that were first published in 1981. John now lives in West Yorkshire and his books of poetry include *Incy-Wincy Moo-Cow* and *A Collection of Weird and Wacky Nursery Rhymes* (Hodder Wayland).

Peter Dixon

Peter Dixon grew up in London during the Blitz, and readily admits to being a rather naughty boy whose schooling was far from successful. He tended to write secretly at home . . . drawing and writing of things for school was largely ignored. As an adult, Peter became a soldier for two years and detested every moment; he then became a teacher and a lecturer in education. He is married and has two children. Peter's books include *Grow Your Own Poems*

(Peche Luna), *Lost Property Box* (with Wes Magee and Matt Simpson, Macmillan) and Peter Dixon's *Grand Prix of Poetry* (Macmillan).

Andrew Fusek Peters

When Andrew Fusek Peters was at school he was bullied and poetry became a good way of getting revenge on the page. Now that he is six foot eight in height he no longer suffers from bullying, but he does still write poetry. "I write my poems under a tree high up in the Shropshire Hills or in my study if it's cold!" He has appeared on 'Blue Peter', 'The Big Breakfast' and was a writer-presenter on 'Wham Bam Strawberry Jam'. His books include, *Poems With Attitude* (Hodder Wayland) – a teenage poetry collection written with his wife Polly Peters and the anthologies, *The Upside Down Frown* – a book of shape poems (Hodder Wayland) and *The Barefoot Book of Strange and Spooky Stories*.

David Orme

David Orme is an avid science fiction fan as well as a poet and anthologist. He was born in Stoke but moved south with his family when he was two. He now lives in Winchester. David has written over a hundred books but his teacher once told his parents that he would never achieve anything as he couldn't get anything down on paper! When he isn't writing, David visits schools to talk about his writing. He is married to Helen and they have two grown up sons. David's books include volumes of his own poetry *The Gravedigger's Sandwich* (KQBX) and *Heroes and Villains* (Pearson), anthologies *They Think it's all Over* (Macmillan) and *Nothing Tastes Quite like a Gerbil* (Macmillan), and an autobiography *Losing My Roof* (Collins Pathways).

Joan Poulson

Joan Poulson has been a writer for a radio 'soap', a television cook, and had a 15-minute play performed in a Manchester theatre.

Her poetry has been sculpted in stone and has formed part of a modern dance performance. Many of her ideas arrive from swift, strong connections between one thing – something she sees, reads, overhears, and another – an advert on a bus, a dog running down the street, a photograph. "With the connection comes a spark – and a compulsion to write." Joan's most recent books for children are *Girls are Like Diamonds* (OUP) and *Pictures In My Mind* (Hodder Wayland).

Coral Rumble

For Coral Rumble, poetry is the fascinating challenge of word juggling. "The poet must choose words carefully and then 'throw' them with skilful precision, so that the magic and the rhythm and good timing keeps them all in the right place." She used to be an English teacher and now works in schools providing workshops for all ages. She often does her writing at the local library to get away from the phone! Coral's first collection of poetry for children *Baboons' Bottoms* (Initiative Press) was published in 1995. A recent collection is *Creatures, Teachers and Family Features* (Hodder Wayland).

Nick Toczek

Nick Toczek is a performance poet, storyteller, magician, puppeteer and comedian. He is married with two children and lives in Bradford where he was born in 1950. Nick has been a full-time performer and writer for thirty years during which time he has published more than 25 books, has done over 20,000 performances and worked with pupils from about 2,500 schools. "I write every day, it's my job . . . I write anywhere and everywhere." Nick's books include *Dragons* and *Dragons Everywhere* (Macmillan), *Never Stare at a Grizzly Bear* (Animal poems, Macmillan) and *Can Anyone Be as Gloomy as Me?* (Hodder Wayland).

Acknowledgements

The Publishers would like to thank the following publishers and illustrators who allowed us to use their material in this book:

Barefoot Books for *Someone I Like* (Giovanni Manna); Keith Brumpton for *Boneyard Rap* (Hodder Wayland); Faber & Faber for *The Mermaid's Purse* (Flora McDonnell); Shirley Felts for *Dragonsfire* (Faber & Faber); Frances Lloyd for *Strawberry Drums* (Hodder Wayland); Claire Mackie for artwork from *Michael Rosen's Book of Nonsense Poems* (Hodder Wayland); Macmillan Children's Books, London, for *Fruits* (David Axtell); Eunice McMullen/Charles Fuge for *Bears don't Like Bananas* (Hodder Wayland); Oxford University Press for *Four o'Clock Friday* (Nick Sharratt); Puffin (Penguin Books Ltd) for *Bad Bad Cats* (Linda Monks), *Lunch Boxes don't Fly* (Korky Paul), *Madtail, Miniwhale and Other Shape Poems* (Caroline Crossland), *The Puffin Book of Magic Verse* (Emma Shaw-Smith), *Smile, Please!* (Jean Baylis), *Talking Turkeys* (Janet Woolley); Kelly Waldek for *I Wish I could Dine with a Porcupine* (Hodder Wayland).

For photographs: Egmont Children's Books 6; Puffin 9 (David Hills), 29, (Phil Polglaze); Faber & Faber 13 (Caroline Forbes); Ivor Fields Photographic 11; Steve Rice 25; David Silliton 19; Wiltshire Times 23.

Faber & Faber for permission to use the poem *Woodpecker* by Ted Hughes.

We would also like to thank 'Books for Keeps' magazine for permission to quote from some of their 'Authorgraphs'.

More information about poets can often be found in this bimonthly journal and their publication 'A Guide to Poetry 0-13' is invaluable. For details write to Books for Keeps, 6 Brightfield Road, Lee, London SE12 8QF. Tel: 0181 852 4953.
E-mail: booksforkeeps@btinternet.com

Also thanks to 'Young Writer' for permission to quote from their Michael Rosen interview. 'Young Writer' is a specialist magazine for young writers from 6-16, featuring interviews with top children's writers plus many chances for children to see their own prose and poetry in print. Three issues are published per year. Contact 'Young Writer', Glebe House, Weobley, Herefordshire HR4 8SD. Tel: 01544 318901. Web site: http://www.mystworld.com./youngwriter

A Teachers' Poetry Information Pack: Poetry for the Classroom – which gives details of poetry competitions for children, poetry events in schools, bookshops selling children's poetry and much more, may be obtained free by writing to The Poetry Library, Level 5, Royal Festival Hall, London SE1 8XX.

Further information about the poets included in this book may be found on publishers' websites e.g. Puffin at http://www.puffin.co.uk

Macmillan at http://www.panmacmillan.com

and for Brian Moses on http://www.poetryzone.ndirect.co.uk

Most of the poets in this book are regular visitors to schools and may be contacted via the publicity departments of their publishers.